MW00903102

Break The Chain!

SMT: Strong Mind Training

How to Create Money, Love, Health and Happiness

Joseph L. Hurtsellers - Sensei

Book 1

**Copyright © 2015, 2016 by
Joseph L. Hurtsellers**

For Complete Information about Sensei Joseph Hurtsellers and his dojo please visit:

www.ohiomartialarts.com

Dedication

Much of what is written in this book was learned from my many teachers. Some I've had the privilege to meet personally. Others have taught me through books, recordings and seminars.

But the best teaching is always done through example. No teacher has influenced me more than my life partner:

Shelly Blanco.

Shelly has the uncanny ability to take difficult situations, hard work, and challenges and somehow make them all fun.

She has taught me that every solution comes with a smile.
Every breakthrough comes from joy.
Every conquest comes with a twinkle in the eye.

Thank you Shelly for being my Mary Poppins.

Why I Wrote This Book

From the time I was fifteen I did everything they told me. I got up early, I worked hard, I took risks. But thirty years later I was broke, tired, and inside I felt dead.

Most of those thirty years I spent struggling. Never quite succeeding; never quite doing poorly enough to quit - just enough to get by. I could seriously relate to the character Desmond on the TV show "Lost"who had to push a sequence of buttons every 108 minutes or the world would end. Desmond barely lived his life. I didn't live much of mine either.

For thirty years I listened to the advice of others and stayed close to my business. Not making enough to be secure, not losing enough to stop. I stayed.

… and listened.

… and listened.

… to others.

Finally I STOPPED listening.

I stopped listening to what other people said. Instead I started to pay attention to me.

What I'm going to show you in this book is the result of what happened when I stopped listening to other people and started to pay attention to my inner voice.

This book is about what I learned that got me out of the race. I wrote it to myself; to the me I was all those years ago. It's written for that young man I was with decades of struggle ahead. I'm desperately wishing that he knew then what I know now.

But this book is also written for you; so that wherever you are in life you can benefit from my many years of trial and error. That you too can unlock the door to your prison cell; and walk into the light of day.

During those years of struggle I mostly lived without joy. I bought into the idea that if I sacrificed my joy today then I could have a better tomorrow. Little did I know that the only way out of the trap is THROUGH joy. Joy becomes the most powerful weapon when you know how to focus.

I wrote this book to show you how to find your joy; not in some theoretical or philosophical way. But instead with a step by step system that will show you how.

Along the way I learned that most of what I had been told about success was wrong. I discovered new ways of focusing that will allow anyone to change their life for the better; not in thirty years - but today.

I organized these techniques and put them into a system of meditation and daily habits. That system is called SMT (Strong Mind Training). SMT became the backbone of the philosophy and style of Martial Art I now teach.

As I used the techniques covered here my life improved dramatically:

- For decades I struggled with money. My struggle ended. Now I have more than I need.

- For years I had relationship issues. Those issues are gone forever.

- For decades I was unhappy. Today I've learned how to create my own happiness. I'm going to show you how to be happy.

The book you now hold in your hand was written under the direct influence of the daily work I do with SMT. During its writing I told no one about it; not even my closest family and friends. This book literally wrote itself in silence.

I wrote this for the young man I was over thirty years ago, stepping out for the first time into family life and business. But this was also written for you; so that wherever you are on your journey it can be better. When you use the ideas here you will get more of what you want and find more joy along the way.

You are only inches away from the light of freedom. I'm here to give you a nudge; to help you step fully into the brightness of your power.

Like all teaching; when I see you succeed I will gain more success myself. We are in this together.

This book was written for us.

Why You Should Read This Book

This book will help you if any of the following are true...
Have you noticed people not working nearly as hard as you but getting ahead?

- Have you been stuck (financially, emotionally or otherwise) and wanted to move to a higher level?

- Have you struggled with your emotions of fear, anger or despair?

- Have you followed advice from others but gotten very little results?

You will learn the hidden secrets to why some succeed but most fail. It will teach you a system of daily habits that will unlock the power of your mind; so that you can win the life you want.

Most Success Books Fail

Why is it, with all the success books available today, most people still fail?

Most of the time when things don't work out it's the reader that's blamed. You just didn't apply yourself. You needed more discipline. You should have given more effort. The same people who are blamed for not having enough discipline and hard work then buy books on those subjects; but those books don't work either.

Most books don't work because they point you in the wrong direction. Success has nothing to do with effort. Instead effort comes as evidence of your inspiration.

For years you've been pushing and pushing on the door of success. What a shock to realize that the door you've been pushing on opens to the INSIDE!

Most books turn your attention outside. They give you a map to follow. But the real secret is learning to turn your attention INSIDE. You must learn how to look inside so that you can discover your own unique way of doing things. Not with just theory; but with real practices that make all the difference.

You don't need me or anyone else to tell you WHAT to do. The world is moving so fast that anything you read will be out of date before you finish this book. Instead you need TOOLS to help you figure out where you are blocked. You don't need better character traits. *You need to be unleashed from what's holding you back.*

Inside of you is a unique GPS system. As long as you listen to others it is impossible to follow your own guidance. This book will show you how to stop the constant voices from outside and follow the only voice you can trust - your own.

This book is not simply a philosophy; it contains the actual techniques I used to improve my life. These processes don't just work some of the time; they work ALL the time and for EVERYONE.

Read and study this material. When you put to use the techniques contained here I promise your life will improve - *faster and easier than you ever thought possible.* This book will show you how to release whatever has been holding you back.

Buckle your seat belt. You are about to move quickly.

Table Of Contents

CHAPTER 1: Elephant On A Rope

What's Holding You Back?

In India there is a story about an elephant who is held only by a clothesline to a tiny stake. A man asks the owner "How is it that such a giant animal can be held by such a tiny rope?"

The owner replied: "When he was a little calf he was tied with a steel chain. His will was strong back then. He pulled at the chain over and over again. After thousands of tries he gave up. Today he could walk away at any moment; but he refuses to even try".

I believe we are all like that elephant. We've tried so many times to reach our goals and failed that sometimes we just gave up.

We are no longer pulling at the chain. We don't realize that the world around us has changed. WE have changed. Even a small amount of effort today could make our dreams come true.

As life goes on - like the Elephant - we begin to lie to ourselves. We tell ourselves: "I really don't know what I want". Or "I don't NEED more" and "I don't WANT more". We hide behind our distractions. We use anything and everything as an excuse so we don't have to deal with the risk of failure.

But deep down we know there is something more. Every one of us knows that we were put here for something greater. We just we stopped trying.

If you've started to give up; I'm going to make a bold prediction. By the end of this book your confidence will return. You'll start looking at the rope that's been holding you back with doubt. You'll be wondering just how strong it is.

By the end of this book - you are going to pull. When you pull - just a little - the stake is going to pop out of the ground. You will see how everything you've ever wanted really is still within your reach.

By the then you will be well on your way to reaching your goals. Best of all - it's going to be fun.

The Courage To Be Selfish

The flight attendant says it best: "Put your oxygen mask on first before helping others".

Be selfish; because by putting yourself first you put yourself in a position to bless others.

Don't listen to anyone who tells you to be "unselfish". Don't listen when they tell you to give up what you want for a "greater cause". When someone asks you to give up what you want it's because they want you to become a part of what THEY want.

I'm looking at my crystal ball. It's going to tell me what you are looking for in life.

It's becoming clearer... clearer... clearer. There it is - I can see it now!

You want money. You want freedom. You want love. You want joy.

All of these wants are selfish.

You're selfish.

It's OK.

Selfishness is a sign that your mind is healthy.

Selfish; in that even the most noble thing you do, is still ultimately about you. You are looking for the feeling of freedom; the feeling of joy. Everything you do is so that you can find that selfish sense of joy you're after. It is and always has been about you.

Saints and sinners are alike in one way. They both want more of what we call "joy". But the way they go about getting it is radically different. You are not good or evil based on what you want. You become good or evil based on HOW you get it.

If you want a promotion, a better house, or if you want to help feed a hungry tribe in Africa - we are all in the same boat. We are goal setters and we experience joy when we begin to achieve our dreams.

Joy is your life's work. When you commit yourself to joy you will begin to live radically different. Most people don't think they can achieve their goals. They don't really believe they can be happy. They settle on survival and learn to endure instead of learning to live.

Most people spend their lives getting through things. They get through their day, they get through their week, they get through their years. But when you master the material in this book you will no longer try and get through life; instead you will begin each day and get something FROM it.

Listen to yourself. What do you want? What are you here to do?

When you learn to listen to yourself not only will you know how to be happy; you will have everything you need to reach your goals.

The Path Of Least Resistance

So why is it that so many of us never achieve our goals? What is it that's holding us back? I'm going to show you a group of techniques so powerful that your life will never be the same. The system is composed of two practices that when combined are known as SMT (Strong Mind Training).

The first form of practice is called "Passive SMT". It's designed to eliminate the obstacles in your way. In many cases all you need to do is eliminate the obstacles and life gets better quickly.

The other form of practice is called "Active SMT" and it will teach you to refine your goal setting skills. Techniques found in "Active SMT" will help you focus so that you can directly visualize and manifest the things you want.

This book is about the *first* form of practice "Passive SMT". Passive SMT is the most powerful of the two because it allows you to get the biggest improvements right away. My second book on "Active SMT" will teach you to take what you learn here and supercharge it to move to even higher levels.

Before I dive deeper into the system, let's talk about what's holding you back.

The reason you don't get results is because of false beliefs about success. Most people struggle because they have bought into the lie that successful people have more discipline, are smarter, or have a skill others don't.

Success is not about invisible character traits. Success comes by following very visible principles. Anyone can learn these principles;

and when you use them with consistency you will get consistent results.

For centuries no one in Europe dared to cross the ocean. People lived under an illusion. They looked at the horizon and assumed that that line was where the earth ended. It was obvious. You could see it. The horizon line was proof.

In the same way there are things you now believe true that are completely false. You witness powerful evidence for your false beliefs. But you are drawing the wrong conclusions.

The biggest lie of all is that success is determined by effort.

Because you believed this lie you stayed in your comfort zone for too long - not because you wanted to - but because you DIDN'T EVEN KNOW YOU WERE IN A COMFORT ZONE!

You were born into a world where you were taught that goals are accomplished by hard work! "No pain no gain", and "When the going get tough, the tough get going". But the ability to endure pain should never have been a measure of greatness. More often than not, the ability to endure pain is a measure of stupidity.

But we weren't being stupid; we were just following a bad formula passed on from generation to generation. This formula was most likely passed down to us by a society trying to squeeze more productivity out of its factory workers.

Be a cog in a machine. Don't think for yourself. Don't make your own decisions. Above all don't stand out! That's what your education was based on.

Every now and then someone would follow the old formula; and against all odds STILL succeed. And what happens then? They become a hero! They are put on a pedestal and everyone is told they are the model. We give them awards, statues are made; and some of them even wrote books.

So of course you believed what you were told.

You couldn't possibly have known you were being manipulated.

And just like our baby elephant you pulled and pulled on that chain. You tried and tried. But no matter how much you stayed stuck.

Oh, you might have gotten the stake to move a little every now and then. But mostly - no matter how hard you tried - it didn't move.

You only behaved this way because you were misled. You believed success needed the same skill as the factory - hard work and muscle. But the chain is too strong for muscle. You can only break free when the chain is weak.

You don't need more muscle. You need a hacksaw.

The chain only exists because of a belief in your mind. It can only be removed with the strength of your MIND.

You will learn two things; first how you unconsciously created mental blocks that are preventing you from reaching your goals. Second how to recognize and eliminate those blocks. When the blocks are gone you will move forward quickly and break free.

If you follow these ideas your life will change for the better. You will no longer be a prisoner of "the way it's always been" you will no longer be a captive of chance. You will have shifted the odds in your favor.

When you master SMT practice you will have turned the table on life. You will move from the betting side of life to the dealers side. The odds of success will have shifted in your favor. The more you play the more you win.

The Right Tools

"A hand without tools can get very little work done.
A mind without tools can do very little thinking." - Anonymous

Why is it that one person can run 5 miles with no problem; but another can't go 100 yards? It's simple. One of them practiced.

But if I ask you the question: "Why is it that some people are achieving their goals when others don't?" Almost no one would say it was because of a SKILL that's been practiced.

There is a whole list of things we think are the reasons for success. We THINK this list is true because these items are present when someone accomplishes a goal. *But correlation is NOT causation.*

The items below are not the cause of success; instead they are the RESULT!!

- Hard work
- Perseverance
- Passion
- Self - Discipline
- Luck

I remember when I was in grade school; I hated it. I used to fake stomach aches so I could stay home. School felt like a prison.

Teachers used to roll their eyes at me. Counselors used to tell me I needed more self discipline. No one knew my family situation.

We were literally on the run from the law. We would move to a new place sometimes for only for a few weeks and leave in the middle of the night. I was surrounded by poverty and abuse.

No wonder I hated school. I didn't want to commit. I was afraid. I could lose anything I worked for at any moment. Better to just stay home and hide.

Sometimes I felt jealous of other kids. I used to think; "Of course they work hard and show up. They have a neighborhood. They have houses with yards. They have parents".

No amount of effort. No amount of coaching. No amount of punishment would change my behavior. The only thing that would have helped me would have been to live in a more successful environment.

That's the thing; when a person starts to succeed they really get motivated. *But motivation comes FROM success; not success from motivation.*

There is something that all successful people are doing that you are not. When you learn to do what successful people do you begin to achieve your goals. When you start getting more of what you want life starts to get fun - and when life is fun motivation is easy!

I struggled in school because of a bad environment. People struggle with goals because of a bad MENTAL environment.

SMT is a system I use every day to construct a positive mental environment. SMT techniques have improved my business, my relationships, my lifestyle and my bank account.

SMT is the tool I've used to write every word of this book.

No muscle here. No pain. No punishing self discipline...

...only joy.

Main Ideas Of Chapter 1

- Your limiting thoughts and beliefs are holding you back. You were trained in these limitations since childhood.

- Every person is seeking the same thing. We all want joy.

- Joy is your life's work. Meaningful movement toward your goals creates joy.

- Character traits we erroneously believe are the cause of success are instead the *result* of success.

- The right tools along with practice creates the right environment. You will prosper in the right environment.

- SMT is divided into two sections, Passive and Active. This book will teach the Passive part of the system.

- The results of Passive SMT will be rapid and immediate.

CHAPTER 2: The Foundation of SMT

Passive And Active SMT

In SMT there are many exercises. It is the combination of these techniques that will give you the best results. I use the term meditation; to describe any technique or process that helps you focus your mind. SMT is not one exercise; but instead a variety of methods.

All of these forms of practice are designed to do one thing. To direct your mind away from what you don't want and toward what you do.

Some of these forms of SMT meditation are active (you actually do something positive). Other forms are passive (you stop yourself from doing something negative).

At first it seems like the active practice is most important because you can see a direct cause and effect between your work and the results. But it really is the passive part of SMT that lays the foundation and makes the active part possible. It's like building a house; no matter how big and beautiful you make it, the foundation makes everything else work.

All SMT meditations are simple, easy, and free, but they do require self discipline. As you work with passive SMT your life will improve - often dramatically. Seemingly unconnected relationships, health issues, and even financial situations will improve.

"Luck favors the prepared mind". - Louis Pasteur

SMT is training your mind for good fortune. When good fortune arrives do not pass it off as luck. It is not luck; instead it is what *always* happens when you practice these skills.

Discipline yourself to stay with the practice; even *after* things improve. Do the work every day so that good can continue to come to you every day. Build a foundation on consistency and your world will continue to bloom.

SMT is like the various styles of Martial Arts. Some are better in certain situations; so to be a well rounded Martial Artist it's good to be versed in more than one style. Likewise, SMT training includes a variety of different techniques, but they are all designed to lead you to the same result.

Just like the Martial Arts I teach; techniques can and do change based on new knowledge and changing circumstance. SMT is flexible in the same way; the techniques you learn here are a beginning point, but there will always be more techniques as SMT continues to grow and improve.

SMT is not a dogma. SMT is about finding what works best to get you results.

Law of Attraction (LOA)

"If you live right things happen right." - Walt Disney

SMT is based on a principle often called "Law of Attraction". Law of attraction simply states, you get more of what you focus on. When you focus on gratitude, kindness and joy you get more of those things. When you let yourself give energy to anger, revenge and hate you get more of that too.

Some people criticize Law of Attraction. Usually criticism of LOA comes from people who really don't understand it.

Some say: "It's not about what you think; it's what you do that counts". But this is a misunderstanding of the Law of Attraction. LOA is not so much about what you "think" instead it's about where you choose to focus. Critics don't realize that thought is a very tiny component of LOA - the real power is *focus*.

Imagine a panicking crowd during a fire; lot's of action is taking place - but the action makes things worse! It's only when there is FOCUS that people can get out safely. *LOA is not about inaction; instead it is about focusing properly so you take the RIGHT action.*

No one can really fully control what they think. Thoughts come and go all the time. They come from what you hear, see, smell and touch; they also rise from our memories. In order to control your thinking you would have to totally control your environment. Good luck with that!

Millions of people have been murdered because one group or another wanted to control others. But in the words of the rock band "The Who": *"The new boss is the same as the old boss."*

No one ever wins a battle. The very act of battle creates an environment of fighting. No matter who "wins" something always comes up that can't be controlled. More force is needed forever.

New age philosophers come around and say; "Since you can't control others, you should learn to control your thinking". But our thinking is equally impossible to control with force.

Every thought that has ever been released is floating around, waiting for one of us to pay attention to it. When you try and control your thinking it's impossible. This is because most of the thoughts that occur to you didn't even originate with you in the first place!

Even the most powerful minds in the world cannot fully control their thinking.

If you asked a Zen master NOT to think of a pink elephant; what would he see? Of course - a pink elephant. If results come from thinking, Zen monasteries might be filled with pink elephants!

The greatest Martial Artist of the 20th century - Morie Ueshiba was asked how he was able to stay in perfect physical balance over the previous twenty years. Ueshiba said: *"I lose balance all the time - many hundreds of time each day - but you never notice my loss of balance. This is because I have mastered the art of QUICK RECOVERY".*

And that's the solution. Recovery.

You might not be able to control negative thoughts that come your way. But you do have the power to RECOVER. You have the power to choose where you direct your FOCUS; and your focus determines your results.

Your actions come from your focus

All results follow the same three step process:

1. You choose what to focus on.
2. You focus until you feel emotion.
3. You take action.

Let's take the example of getting a glass of water.

1. First you consider the idea.

2. Next you give the idea more energy by focusing on it. You create in yourself kind of internal "yes" by thinking about how it will look, how it will feel, how refreshing it will taste.
3. Finally you decide; you take action, you get your water.

Each one of the steps is needed to get what you want, but even in this simple example you will notice it's the middle step where most of the work is done. It's the subtle emotional "yes". It's where you focus on the glass of water long enough to almost taste it that makes the difference.

How easy it is to focus is determined by your comfort level. The more discomfort you feel the easier it is. The middle step is where you focus and it's focus that motivates you to take action.

I remember a scene from the TV classic "The Andy Griffith Show". Two of the main characters are sitting on a front porch on a hot North Carolina summer. They chat back and forth in a slow almost poetic southern drawl.

"I think I'm gonna go down to Goobers and get myself a soda".

… pause…

"Yep, good idea; we'll just go down to Goobers get ourselves a soda".

… pause …

"Yep; Gonna go down to Goobers and get a soda".

… pause …

"Yep; Goobers, gonna go down there and get a soda".

It goes on and on, slowly being said; over and over again. But no one *moves*!

It's a funny example of what happens when we have an idea with no emotion behind it. Thoughts without emotion have no energy. When you have a thought; but there isn't enough emotional energy behind it you look LAZY!

But if you stay on a thought long enough; if you work on it for a long enough period of time - it becomes more than just a thought; it begins to generate EMOTION.

If you can imagine smelling the soda, feeling the cool bottle in your hand, tasting how delicious it is, you come to a tipping point. When you feel strong emotion it drives you. If the emotion is strong enough you MUST take action.

When emotion hits you, you have to get up and go to Goobers and buy the damn soda!

No amount of self discipline can cause you to be effective without focus. You might have enough discipline to take action; but the action will be filled with mistakes. You will run out of energy quickly and you will fail. People who are efficient and highly motivated have learned to focus and focus drives their motivation.

To get results don't worry so much about your thinking. Instead give your attention to how you are FOCUSING! When you learn to focus - life will hand you a blank check.

Focus IS Action

Just because you are not doing something physical doesn't mean you're not taking action. On any goal the first action is always focus.

Sometimes I write all day. I'm sitting most of the time. It would be easy for someone to accuse me of laziness. It doesn't look like I'm getting anything done.

But those days are often my most productive. I'm taking huge step towards my goals.

I could have done physical labor during these days. But instead my writing forces my mind to focus. The more focused I am the more effective my actions.

Focus first; then take a tiny physical step in the direction of your goal. But always focus first; otherwise you might step in the wrong direction.

Action does make you feel better in the short term; but only focused actions make you feel better long term.

When you're angry at someone; short term you will feel better if you punch them in the nose. Long term you've made a huge mistake.

Don't punch anyone in the nose. Don't sign on the dotted line. Don't eat the whole bag of potato chips.

Focus first.

Bad Math

This is the formula often mistakenly use to describe the LOA:

Thought + Focus + Actions = Results

This formula is flawed. It's flawed because not all the variables are equal. LOA's formula is not a linear math problem; instead it's more like a RECIPE!

In a recipe the *amount* of each ingredient is critical.

If the recipe for LOA was in a cookbook it might look like this:

RECIPE TO CREATE YOUR REALITY

INGREDIENTS
- **Thought:** Only a Pinch
- **Focus:** 1 to 10 Gallons (the more the better)
- **Action:** 5 Ounces (Use sparingly based on inspiration).

Stir until you get desired result.
THE MORE FOCUS ADDED THE LESS ACTION NEEDED

It's not the thoughts you think that make up your life. It's the thoughts you focus on that have power. You don't succeed through "positive thinking"; you only succeed with positive FOCUSING. Let focus direct your actions.

Where are you spending your focus?

Each day you only get a certain amount of focus. It's like a type of money; how you spend it is up to you. If you are not getting the results you want; it means you've been making poor spending choices.

When you first start to understand Law of Attraction it might seem hard. If you're like me, you probably picked up some bad habits. You learned to fight against all the things in your life you didn't like; not realizing that *all struggle is also a form of focus spent in the wrong direction.* The harder you tried the worse of a hole you dug.

Focus is the main ingredient in achieving a goal. SMT will teach you techniques that will make you an expert at focus.

Main Ideas Of Chapter 2

- Passive SMT (this book) lays the foundation for Active SMT (Found in book 2).

- When you get results do not pass them off as luck.

- There are a variety of evolving techniques that make up SMT.

- SMT is based on often the misunderstood Law of Attraction.

- A desire without focus (emotion) leads to procrastination, and laziness.

- Emotion is created with strong focus. Positive emotions lead to positive results.

- Focus is the most important ingredient in achieving goals.

CHAPTER 3: The Brink

Stop Doing It

Bad old joke: Man says to the Doctor: "It only hurts when I do this."

Doctor replies: "Then don't do that!"

Stop.

Stop doing things that hurt you and life gets better.

Internal SMT teaches that most of the things you want in life will come to you naturally. The reason they aren't here now is because you are using most of your energy focusing on their opposite.

Feeling fear, anger, worry, and complaining are all examples of focusing on what you don't want. The more you feel negative emotions; the more events like them you will attract. Remember what all advertising companies have known for decade; your decisions will always match how you feel.

People spend day after day focusing on what they don't want. They get angry at the government, weather, traffic or something else. They complain. They gripe. They join groups to fight against all sorts of things. But they don't realize they will keep getting more of what they struggle against. Struggle is a powerful form of focus.

When you begin to attract negatives you create a downward spiral. You focus on a negative and get a negative result. Then you fight your result and end up focusing on the negative more.

Believe me. I've been there.

The more you argue and fight against something, the more of it you get. But you can learn to stop your momentum; you can reverse it.

Internal SMT is a lot like the martial art of Jiu-Jitsu. In Jiu-Jitsu you learn to relax and let your partner do the work. Your opponent traps themselves. You don't try and force your moves on the other person; you go where they go, and use their energy against them.

When you practice internal SMT you learn where you are tensing up, where you are resisting. When you stop resisting your life improves quickly - sometimes in startling ways.

Who Do You Hang Out With?

Lab studies have shown you can take a rat that's addicted to a substance; and put it in a cage with a group of rats who are not, and the addicted rat will be CURED! Cured; not with a medication, not with an intervention, but by simply changing the group the rat lives with.

You are the average of your five closest friends.

Think of the five closest people you know. Average their income, and you will have a close estimate of how much you make. You are also the average of your friend's health, relationships, education and everything else.

This rule also applies to our emotions. Take a look at your most common emotions. Which emotions are you closest "friends" with? There is no escaping it; *your life will be the average of the feelings you experience most often.*

If you want life to get better you've got to upgrade your friends - but not just your friends in the physical world. Even more importantly, you've got to upgrade the emotions you have grown to be friendly with.

Your emotions are habitual. Your emotions come from what you choose to focus on. When you practice focusing on something often enough, emotion will rise in you so quickly you won't know where it came from. But strong emotions always come from the same place. *They come from the thoughts you practice holding for long periods of time.*

What Sets You Off?

Almost everyone has a touchy subject. Something (or someone) has caused you so many problems that every time you think of it it sets you off. How did you get to that point?

Usually it started with a problem.

You fought against the problem.

It got worse.

You fought more.

Worse still.

You didn't realize you cannot fight against anything without focusing on a negative emotion.

When you allow yourself to hold onto a thought long enough it generates a negative emotion. You get good at what you practice. If you practice enough your responses become automatic. Eventually (because of practice) every time your problem comes up you quickly feel the emotions you've rehearsed.

Your emotions always affect the decisions you make. Every time you practiced a negative emotion you were programming yourself to make poorer and poorer decisions.

In the early stages these emotions had to take a lot of work to bring to the surface. You have to think, talk and focus on something a lot to create the emotion. But each time you create the emotion it took less and less effort. With practice you got to the point where the least little thing can set you off.

I remember when I went through my divorce. It was so painful and so drawn out (and I gave it so much negative energy) I became an expert in feeling bad. I could be walking on a beach on a sunny day and see a couple holding hands and BOOM - I'd feel a terrible negative emotion sweep over me.

Today I know that the depression and anxiety were just states of mind I had learned through practice. I learned to stop hurting myself. It was practice that got me into my mess; and it was practice that got me out.

Practice is what causes you to feel good or bad. Emotions do not just happen; emotions come from what you practice. Practice well and you will live well.

Several years ago I read an article about Tibetan Monks who could control their biological systems during meditation. They could speed up or slow down their pulse, blood pressure, even the chemicals that the brain created in their bodies.

I wonder if anyone realized it. That's what we are all doing every day. Every thought you focus on, good or bad, is a meditation. Focus on joy; and you release joyful chemicals. Focus on fear; and you release chemicals that make you afraid.

Focus on a thought of fear right now and notice what happens to your heart rate, your respiration, your entire metabolism. This isn't just something monks can do; you do it all the time.

What Are You On The Brink Of

Imagine you are in the mountains sitting on safe ground. Fifty yards in front of you is the edge of a cliff. But you are safe; you're not even close to the edge. The view is nice from your spot.

It's on this safe ground that we usually start off our day. But every time you focus on things you don't want you nudge yourself closer and closer to the edge. Every time you complain, every time you gripe, every time you accuse, you've taken another step towards the edge.

When you are on the edge all it takes is one more thought, one more event, one more reminder and… BAM! You lose control. You say and do things you don't mean. You become a danger to yourself and others. You are in a free fall.

Have you ever heard people say words like:

- *"Just one more thing and I'm gonna lose it"!*

- *"I'm on the verge of a nervous breakdown"!*

- *"I'm on the verge of a heart attack"!*

There's a terrible truth about these statements. The person speaking them is RIGHT!

But how does someone get to the point where they are so close to the edge? They got there one push, one nudge, one step, at a time.

Here's a key: The push is when you think about a subject; the FORCE behind the push is when you hold onto it long enough to feel a negative emotion. In other words it's not your thought - it's your decision to STAY on it - that gives it pushing power.

Here's another key: Every time you start to feel the push of a negative emotion - no exceptions - you will feel bad!

This negative emotion is your own private "spider sense". It's telling you that danger is near. You are about to step in the wrong direction.

When you practice paying attention to your "spider sense" it grows stronger. You will begin to spot trouble before it starts. You will begin to avoid problems before they get out of control.

The art of paying attention to your emotions is known as mindfulness. To master SMT then, you've got to be a master of mindfulness. You've got to practice being aware of your feelings enough to catch yourself and change your thought every time you start to feel bad.

In other words: SMT is the art of feeling good.

One Pointedness

Begin by being aware of your emotions. Ask yourself dozens of times a day; "How do I feel right now?" Watch for any negative emotions and try and figure out where they are coming from. Instead of trying to change the negative into a positive, simply focus your attention on something else that makes you feel better.

Teaching young kids has taught me how to focus. If I've got ten kids in a class and one starts to misbehave, if I start trying to correct him the others nearby will misbehave too. Pretty soon the whole class is unfocused; and it's because of ME. It's because I directed my attention in the wrong place.

Instead I give my attention to the nine who are focused. I compliment them, I praise them (especially in front of the child who is not paying attention). Almost always the student who is unfocused joins the rest of the group. It's all about where I put my energy.

Shift your attention away from the things that get under your skin. Instead place your attention on the things you love, that give you joy, that make you happy.

In Zen the process of focusing on what you choose and excluding other things is called: "one pointedness". One pointedness is the purpose of virtually all forms of meditation. One pointedness is what we are developing with the techniques found in SMT.

Catch Yourself Early

When you catch your thought early (before you are falling off a cliff) you can change them and stop their energy. With the awareness of how you feel and practice - you can prevent most negative emotion.

You can practice yourself into better and better feeling thoughts - to the point where you can then begin to push yourself in the OPPOSITE direction!

You can push yourself to a place where you are right on the edge of another cliff. On the new cliff you will be saying things like: ...

- *"If that happens one more time I think I'm going to fall in love!"*

- *"Just one more thing and I'm going to burst into joy!"*

- *"I'm right on the verge of ... the happiest moment of my life!"*

It's learning to push yourself in the RIGHT direction that is the point of "External" SMT - and we'll cover that in book two. *But the external part of the practice only works when you learn the internal part.* For most people; when you stop sabotaging yourself and learn to stop negative emotion your entire world will change for the better - fast.

Often when you learn to stop negative emotion things get so much better that you don't need to do anything else. You will just let your life unfold naturally in pleasant ways. *Stopping your negative emotions might be the only thing you need.*

What's Your Point Of Attraction?

People ask me all the time how to tell their point of attraction. I've heard people say you should look at the life you're living, and the results you're getting as your indication of your focus.

I hate that answer.

It's might be good advice if things are going great. But if your life sucks it's terrible.

If your life sucks, and you look at it sucking - it will make you feel bad. Feeling bad is a point of focus that will make your life suck even more.

In other words, if you are stuck in quicksand, it's time to stop kicking and sinking deeper. There is nothing inside the quicksand that will save you. You've got to find a rope, a branch, anything - OUTSIDE the quicksand that can pull you out. Your answer is never in the hole you already dug.

"A problem can never be solved at the same level of thought that created it." - Einstein

Telling someone to look at the results they are getting in life to determine their point of focus is like telling a golfer that they can tell how good they are by looking at the scorecard. Duhhhh... jeez - like wow; I had no idea!

If you wanted to improve your golf game you would take lessons. A coach would teach you specific things you could do to improve. When you practice specific skills your game will improve.

I'm going to be your coach. I'm going to give you specific techniques I use on a daily basis. These methods have changed my life. They will change yours too.

You now know everything you need to understand and benefit from practices in the rest of this book.

Main Ideas Of Chapter 3

- Stop doing what is hurting you and life gets better.

- You are the average of your five closest friends; your results are the average of your five closest emotions.

- Each emotion you practice pushes you closer to a place where it can completely pull you in. You fall into hatred exactly the same way you fall in love.

- You now have the groundwork to understand the rest of this book.

SMT Exercise: "One Pointedness"

Remember the value in feeling good. Any time you feel a negative emotion rise think of it as your "spider sense". Discipline yourself to turn your attention to a more positive subject. Practice keeping your mind on what you want for longer and longer periods. Do not allow yourself to get distracted by what you don't want.

CHAPTER 4: Kindness - Your Shortcut To Positive Thinking

Superman

A few years ago a major university held a double blind study. Two random groups of people were taken into a room to "test" a video game system. They were given a 3D experience and told they were there to evaluate how accurate they felt the graphics were.

The first group was taken on a trip through nature. They saw a forest, trees, butterflies and so on. But the second group; got to play the part of Superman; flying over cities and smashing through walls.

At the end of the video trial each volunteer was taken into a room with a representative who was there to ask them questions about the game. As the questioner sat down they would "accidentally" tip their pencil cup onto the floor - spilling the pencils everywhere.

You know what was discovered? People who had gotten a chance to play Superman were something like 80% more likely to help pick up the pencils than the other group.

What I'm saying is this - when you are feeling strong and successful, when you are on the right track, when you are reaching your goals, you will automatically be more kind!

When you put your efforts into improving how powerful you feel, your behavior always improves. Put as much effort as you can into the SMT skills that you learn here and your life will improve the first week. Stick with it for a few months; and your life will change forever.

Forgive

It's time to find your power. You find your power by getting rid all those things that are stealing it. *The biggest thief of your personal power is feeling anger or resentment toward anyone or anything.*

Resentment is simply a form of focus. When you resent you are focusing on what you don't want. You are stealing energy which could be used to achieve your goals. The more you resent the more you lose.

A man I know was driving in a crowded city. Another car pulled out in front of him; and caused him to slam on his brakes. My friend got out and started yelling at the guy who cut him off. "Who the BLEEP do you think you are!"

The other driver got a strange look on his face and said: "I'm sorry to tell you this; but I think someone just stole your car".

Sure enough; while my friend was screaming at someone else; a homeless guy jumped in his car and drove away.

Life is like that. Every second you spend in criticism takes your eye off of the things that matter. Every second you resent you invite something bad.

How To Forgive The Past

I get it. Real things have happened to you. You have suffered at the hands of evil. But forgiveness is not about the other person; forgiveness is about *you.*

Your lack of forgiveness will prevent you from reaching your goals.

The other person hurt you in the past; but now it's YOU that is hurting you. When you forgive all you are really doing is making a choice to stop hurting yourself. The other person doesn't deserves your forgiveness; but you deserve it. Forgive for you; no one else.

Here's how I practice forgiveness: I picture the person who has hurt me as a child on Christmas morning getting something they've wanted for a long time. I see their eyes light up, I see them smile, I see them with friends and family and surrounded by the people that love them.

Even though this is just an image in my mind; I know what I'm seeing is REAL. The person who hurt me used to be that child. If the person who hurt me could ever get back to who they were on Christmas morning, I know they would never hurt anyone. I know it's THAT person that they really are.

When my kids we're little they all got to the age when they asked if their is a Santa. I never lie to them; but I always said YES. I said yes because I never stopped believing in the big guy. To me Santa was never a person - he is the magic that happens when we feel love. Santa Claus is the look on the face, that smile, that warm feeling inside that happens when kindness is present.

I have come to realize, that the people we call "evil" are just people who haven't gotten a visit from Santa yet.

Don Miguel Ruiz - in his beautiful little book "The Mastery of Love" uses the example of an injured pet. If your pet is hurt in a certain part of it's body, and you touch it there, it will try and bite you. Not because your pet is evil; but because you are touching it in a place where it hurts.

It's sad that there are so many hurt people walking around today. The pain they feel sometimes makes them want to hurt others. All you can do is remember where they are coming from; it's not personal - for whatever reason, you are just reminding them of the pain they feel inside. You've got to try and remember to see them as they really are - as a child on Christmas.

You might say this is unrealistic; there are real bad things going on today. *But just because something is true doesn't mean it deserves your focus.* There are a lot of true things that I do not want to create more of - so I have a choice. I can focus on something that is "true" that makes me unhappy; or I can choose to focus on what brings me joy. I choose joy.

I'm reminded of one of my favorite quotes; it's from the character; Edward P. Dowd from the classic motion picture "Harvey". In the movie Dowd is thought to be crazy; he see's the world as an amazing and wonderful place, in spite of all the people caught up in their problems.

Dowd says: *"I've wrestled with reality for 35 years Doctor, and I'm happy to state I finally won out over it".*

Dowd was right. The reality we live in is up for grabs. You can tap and let reality win or choose your own reality.
I choose NOT to tap.

As I'm writing this chapter I'm currently going through the threat of litigation. The people who are suing me are trying to use the court system to prosper at my expense. I'm daily sending those others and their attorneys love, and well wishes. I pray for them more than I pray for my closest friends. Every time I send them a sincere prayer for more abundance, health, and joy - I get a surge of love and power that flows through me.

I like the way I feel when I love. I like how powerful it makes me. I think it's the best thing I could do for my health.

I tell myself stories about the people who masquerade as enemies in my life.

The stories I create always try and find a way to prevent me from seeing the other as an opponent. I imagine the other person the day they graduated high school; I wonder how proud their parents felt of them. I invent stories about unknown motivations of good that are beyond my knowing.

I invent stories all for the purpose of drawing me away from negativity and back into love.

It sounds stupid. Someone does something evil and you choose to love? - It's nonsense.

But the money is gone already. There is no getting it back.

She already left you. She took the kids. The pain is almost unbearable.

But the pain you are feeling is not about what happened. The pain is an echo in your mind...

... the only thing that is still hurting you is inside. Your anger, your revenge, your hatred - they are all YOURS. Maybe they are even making you sick. Your wrongdoer can't feel your hatred; only the cells in your body can feel it. They are being damaged.

Forgive And Love

When you love you are not opening yourself up to be a victim. Instead you are immunizing yourself against anything negative in the future.

Love and forgiveness create a field of power around you. Love is an invisible security system. Nothing can touch you when you love.

The Warrior Sage

The Dojo I direct has a logo with a drawing of a warrior sage (wise man) on it. The sage is known as the most powerful warrior, yet he is known as the kindest being. Every time I look at our logo I'm reminded of this quote.

"The sage is kind to the kind, and he is kind to the unkind - because kindness is his nature." - Lao Tzu - 600 BC

Kindness is power; kindness is love.

When you bless the world you bless yourself. People will call you naive; but remember it's only those that are innocent enough to be naive that have pushed humanity forward throughout human history. It's only those who are naive that open themselves up to the power of love.

Have the courage to be the person you once were; the person who was naive, but happy.

Stay focused on your goals and your daily practice - when you begin to see the results of this work you will know it's power. Do everything you can to be more like you were on one of those special holiday mornings long ago.

Stay with love, in the end it's the only thing that matters.

Being kind is not a sign of weakness; it's a sign of power. Be kind, because it's kindness that will light the path to your goals.

Main Ideas Of Chapter 4

- Forgive for what it does for you

- Kindness comes from power

- Anger and resentment steal your power

- Learn to forgive by telling a new story (even if you feel it's untrue) because forgiveness will unleash your power again

- Nothing can hurt you when you truly love

SMT Exercise

- Practice forgiveness. If someone has hurt you try and see them differently. Picture them as a child on Christmas morning. Remember that is who they once were and who they can be again.

- Create stories that support how you want to feel. Ignore whether the stories you make up are true. Joy does not require truth. Joy is a story you tell.

CHAPTER 5: Die Daily

Tonight I am going to die.

Don't worry. It's the the 18,360 time I've died. I'm used to it; it's getting boring.

You've died thousands of times too.

Every time you go to sleep you die. You lose the life that you are living; your consciousness vanishes, and you wake up the next morning born again.

That's a good thing too; because every night you have a chance to decide who you want to be when you are reborn. Every morning you get to decide to live as that new person.

This chapter is about how to go to bed at night so that you can program yourself during that one third, invisible part of your life. Then you will learn how to wake up, and capitalize on each new day to become the person you choose.

The Right Sleep

I recommend sleep. I have found sleep to be as powerful (or MORE powerful) than any form of seated meditation I teach. If you aren't getting at least eight hours of sleep do whatever it takes to make this happen.

I also recommend naps; some of the sharpest minds in the world habitually nap shortly before heavy negotiations. Many professional athletes nap a few hours before a competition. Sleep is not a waste of time - sleep is a shortcut to effectiveness.

Don't believe stories of famous people who got by on very little sleep. Some of the stories are exaggerated or not true. Some stories are about people who were suffering from illness that made sleep difficult. The reality is that successful people who get plenty of sleep vastly outnumbers those that don't. It's not even close.

Sleep is a powerful place to start your SMT training for two reasons:

First; sleep resets you back to a non-resistant state, where all of the negative thoughts and feelings that may arise during the day are gone. No matter where you end up emotionally today; sleep is always there to give you a fresh start to work from tomorrow.

Second; the immediate feeling of well being you experience immediately when you wake teaches you what the non-resistant state you are trying to practice throughout your day will feel like. The feeling you have after sleep is your reference to identify what your after. You will use that feeling to tell when you are on track; and when you are off.

Practice #1: Go To Sleep

The last five minutes before you go to sleep is critical. This is the time when you are programming your mind; this is the time where the information you provide from the conscious world will go with you into the unconscious one. During this last five minutes do everything you can to create the feelings that represent what you want.

If you want more wealth; get the feeling of abundance. If you want more love, get the feeling of being loving. If you want more joy, find the feeling of gratitude. Take these feelings with you as you drift off.

When you can't sleep usually it's because of worry. Your worries only exist when you are being self absorbed. You cannot worry and be thankful at the same time; that's just the way it works.

Practice placing your mind on the things that you are lucky enough to have. If you can't sleep, don't try and count something as useless as sheep; instead do what I do - count at least twenty things you are grateful for. I never make it to twenty; usually I'm out before I even get to ten.

If you practice the feeling of the things you want, if you try to practice gratitude, but still can't sleep don't keep laying there. You don't want to drift off in a disharmonious state and program your unconscious with negativity. Get up, meditate, read something inspirational, do anything you can to get yourself back to the state of harmony before you drift off.

Practice #2: Wake Up

How do you feel when you wake up in the morning?

In the early stages; immediately when you first wake up there is usually a stillness. There is a feeling of peace and comfort; a feeling that says: "Everything is going to be OK". The feeling that everything is basically right with the world is what you are reaching for when you practice SMT.

Where does this sense of well being you feel in the morning come from? It's because during your sleep you we're no longer able to focus on poor habits of focus and negative emotions. Sleep allows you to hit the reset button; to get a fresh start.

Start Your Practice When You Wake

When you first wake; don't move. Don't get out of bed, just lay there quietly and notice how comfortable you are, how good it feels to breath and be alive. Take a few moments and in your mind list all the things you are thankful for. Your life, your home, your friends, your relationships, your dog. Anything and everything you can think of.

Here is one of my favorite quotes; I say it to myself before I get out of bed each day. You might want to use it too:

"I always have a wonderful time, wherever I am, whomever I'm with."
- Elwood P. Dodd from the movie "Harvey"

The first few minutes as you lie awake in bed are setting the tone for your day. You are telling your mind what to focus on and what to look for today. You are setting a goal.

The first step of internal SMT is to make a commitment that today - no matter what tries to pull you off course - you are going to have a wonderful day. You are going to give attention to the things that bring you joy and happiness and you are going to turn away from anything that brings you down.

Sounds simple - and it is. But it won't be without its challenges. The world will try it's best to pull you back in.

If you are brave - and you are - you will learn to ignore the pull of the world and you will learn how to construct a world of your own.

Whoever wins the battle for the world you live in... wins.

Main Ideas of Chapter 5

- Each time you go to bed it's as if you die and are reborn the next morning. It's your second chance for a new life each day.

SMT Exercise

- Get enough sleep (at least eight hours).

- Take special care of the last five minutes before you drift off to be grateful and find joy so that you can take this state into your unconscious.

- When you wake lay in bed a few minutes and remember all that you are grateful for. Then decide to hold onto your feeling of appreciation throughout the day.

CHAPTER 6: Sneak Out the Back

*"The cleanest cut comes from the sword that is never drawn." -
Anonymous Samurai Maxim*

I've spent a year surrounded by hatred.

I bought a condo and downsized from a large house. We bought the condo so we wouldn't have to worry and so we could go trips, and have more freedom.

My first year we were trapped.

The condo we bought is inside a very close community. Only forty units; all units back up to a very public open community patio, pool, entertainment space. Absolutely lovely.

But the culture was filled with hatred, deception, and ugliness.

For unknown reasons, a war between the residents existed. It was like moving into a feud between the Hatfields and McCoys.

My wife and I could not go outside without getting "caught" by one side or the other. Each time we would get approached by another resident they kept trying to pull us to one side or the other. You could feel the hatred in the air.

It got so bad that I would literally draw my curtain and sneak out the back door in order to avoid people that live here.

I can't tell you how hard it was. Both sides were so on edge that if you smiled at one side or the other, the next day you would be confronted by the other side about what you heard or what you said.

I'm no Doctor; but I've noticed the cancer rates in these forty units are unusually high.

We survived that first year. It took some doing but we got through it. A few people moved away, a few resigned from the condo board, a few others started coming outside again.

I want to share with you how we got through it.

Exit Strategy

We did everything we could to not give attention to either side; to not add fuel to the fire. We were nice to others no matter what - in front of them AND behind their backs. (Even when it was just the two of us talking).

Were we perfect? No way - but then again no one was keeping score.

We made plenty of mistakes; but I'm proud to say we did things right far more than we did them wrong. In the end we destroyed no relationships, and truly do love and respect everyone involved.

My wife is now involved heavily with helping the condo board. Why? Because even the people that hated each other like her.

We walked into a battlefield and saw the whole thing flip. It took a year (but if we had done better it would have taken even less time). We have the nicest grounds of any condo in town; and now we have some of the nicest neighbors too.

I know this sounds arrogant. But I'm going to level with you. I think the place changed because of us.

This is the power of sneaking out the back. You can make a big impact on the things around you by what you choose to focus on. It's not easy - because the attraction to get pulled is so strong, but it can be done.

"Sneaking out the back" means refusing to look at your problem; instead you purposely look elsewhere. "Sneaking out the back" is an exit strategy; and the exit strategy for avoiding negative emotion is turning your attention away from negativity toward something you love.

We Are Problem Solvers

Sneaking out the back is hard because we have been trained against it. We have practiced problem solving for year and years. We feel like if we are not being confrontational then we are not getting anything done.

We build monuments to our heroes; every statue is of someone who supposedly won or lost some war. No one ever builds a statue of a person who decided to just live a happy life.

It's the person who lives a happy life, who manages to spend their days having fun, and tries hard to not hurt others that we should be putting on a pedestal. We should build statues of people who choose love.

We are told that good comes from the battles we fight. But in the places where there is war the only people that seem to prosper are those that stir up the trouble.

Politicians gain power, corporations make money, people die. All in the name of problem solving; all in the name of confrontation. If meeting our problems head on worked surely the world would be in better shape?

We got it wrong. We think results come from actions - so we ignore our feelings. We get in fights; we manipulate, we struggle. Sometimes people say we win, other times they say we lose. But either way life gets harder.

We use popular slogans. We say things like:

- When the going gets tough the tough get going!
- Pull yourself up by your own boot straps!
- No pain no gain!

The list goes on. We think if we say something enough it will be true. But two plus two doesn't equal five no matter how many times you say it.

The truth is, you create your own reality. Your reality is created continuously by the emotions you practice, not by effort. When you focus on hate you bring more hatred. When you focus love - you bring more love.

What if there is something in front of you so hateful, so negative that you can't love it?

Sneak out the back door.

This is not the time for confrontation. This is not the time for a solution. This is not the time to make things better. It is time to retreat; you've got to slip out the back.

For decades I felt "stuck" in the Midwest. I'd complain again and again about the weather; every time I felt I had an opportunity to move to a warmer climate something would come up and push back my plans. I felt like George Bailey in "It's a Wonderful Life".

I tried to persevere. I kept trying to love something I really didn't like. I kept trying to look at the climate in Ohio and tell myself it was OK; but for me it wasn't.

Every time I looked at the sky I would get bitter and angry. Every time I tried to think positively about the climate I'd get more and more frustrated. My attempted "positive thinking" was actually keeping me stuck!

Finally I figured it out. I stopped talking about the weather in Toledo - I only talked about the weather in Tucson.

If someone came up to me in Ohio and said: "Ugh; the weather here sure is awful."

I would say: "You should see the weather in Tucson - it's lovely right now!"

Every time I thought about the weather in Toledo I'd feel bad; but every time I thought about the weather in Tucson I'd feel good! I decided I'd rather feel good than bad; so I made Tucson's weather my point of discussion.

Today I still talk about the weather in Tucson - almost every day. Because today; I have a second home in the Catalina Foothills (Just outside of Tucson).

Focusing on what I already loved is what opened the doors and made my move possible. Instead of trying to confront Toledo weather; I took a different path and spent my time focusing on what I wanted instead. In other words I snuck out the back.

This works with people too. If you can't love the evil people that pop up in your life it's OK to stop trying. Instead use the people you ALREADY love to train your emotions. The more you love anything; the more things you love will show up. Eventually the evil ones go away.

Think of your kids, your lover, your best school teacher. Think of your Mom, think of your dog. Think of anyone, or anything you love. Make a list of everyone or everything you love and keep it with you.

When someone confronts you tell them you need to go to the bathroom. (They'll always let you). When you get in the bathroom get out your list and focus.

Focus.

Focus.

Focus ... on all those wonderful people you are in love with.

Focus like your life depends on it.

Remember the words of Donald Shimoda in Richard Bach's classic book: "*Illusions*":

"*There is no problem so big that it can't be walked away from.*"

You solve the world's problems not by fixing them; instead you look at what makes you happy. You become a joyful person, and in just a little time the world around you must become joyful too. This is law.

Negative Thinking Kills

What would happen if you never focused on a negative thought again?

Take a log; place it on the ground, balance on it and walk its length, easy right? Now take the same log and put it between two buildings ten stories up and see what happens.

The question is; why is your balance different at ten stories than when flat on the ground? Because you have introduced an element of danger. That element of danger makes you think about falling. Your negative thought affects your behavior and makes it likely you will fall.

If the technicians from Disney could create the illusion that you were still on the ground - even though you were ten stories up - you would continue to have perfect balance. You lose balance because of your thoughts - not gravity.

Negative thinking will kill you.

Most of life is not so dramatic. You decide on where to live, who to date, what to eat and so on. But each decision you make is dramatically affected by your thinking. When you make decisions out of fear and discomfort you make bad decisions.

The daily practice in SMT is to take each day and do everything you can to keep your mind focused on what you want.

Never look down.

The Fifteen Second Rule

In our home we jokingly have what we call our five second rule; when someone drops a chip on the ground if you pick up it up within five seconds it's OK to eat.

In SMT we have the fifteen second rule. This means that if you have a thought, as long as you stop it within fifteen seconds you will be OK.

It takes about fifteen seconds for a thought to begin to gain momentum. If you stop the thought or change the subject within the first fifteen seconds no damage is done.

Dr. Wayne Dyer used to use the analogy of a ticker tape for stocks that runs along the bottom of your TV screen. This ticker tape represents the thousands of thoughts you have every day. You notice these "thought stocks" as they go streaming by. Just like a real stock you should only buy the ones that are good for your portfolio.

When you hold on to a thought for more than fifteen seconds you have just made a purchase. The longer you hold on to a thought the more you buy. Eventually your life (portfolio) is filled with whatever you have decided to choose to focus on; good or bad.

Only buy into thoughts that you want into your life. You can always tell when a thought is a good investment; it will make you happy, clear, or more loving. You can also always tell when a thought is bad for you - harmful thoughts cause a negative emotion.

Certain daily habits become impossible when you live by the 15 second rule. It's almost impossible to watch the news, read the paper, or argue with anyone.

The 15 second rule is the art of being constantly aware of how you feel during every thought, every conversation, every piece of media that enters into your awareness. Practice learning to quickly discard the unwanted.

Is this an easy practice? No - not at first; you have to work at it; but after a little while it gets easier and easier. The trick is to take one day at a time for at least thirty days. You will fail plenty; but if you will stay at it for thirty days you will see such a massive difference in your life that you will never go back to who you were before.

Use the 15 second rule for one day and you will notice a marked difference in how you feel. Practice it for a month and your life will change. Practice for a year and the lives of those around you will be impacted in unimaginable ways.

Practice the fifteen second rule for the rest of your life and you can change the world. No kidding.

Wipe Down The Sink

Last night I got bit by a mosquito. It's under my watch band on my left side of my wrist.

It feels good when I scratch it. It feels like I'm doing something; but every time I scratch it itches more.

I know that if I stop scratching and just let it alone it will get better.

But it feels so good to scratch.

Thinking of your problems is like scratching a mosquito bite.

For some reason it feels good to think about your problems. Discuss them. Poke at them. Tear at them.

But if you do they will get worse.

It's better to focus your mind somewhere else and leave your own problems alone. A great way to do that is to think of others. It's impossible to worry about your own problems when you're busy helping someone else.

15 years ago I decided to try and make every place I went a little better. If someone needed a compliment I'd just give it. If there was a paperclip on the floor I'd just pick it up. I had been doing this practice for over a year.

One night I took my kids to the movies. I stopped in to use the bathroom and then sat down with them in the theatre seats.

While the previews were playing I started to feel bad. I felt uncomfortable; I didn't know what it was but something was wrong.

It hit me; I had noticed water splashed all over the sink in the bathroom and had walked out without making it better. I told my kids I'd be right back and headed back to the washroom, grabbed a few paper towels and wiped down the sink.

Ahhh… that was better.

A few month later I found myself visiting my brother in the Bethesda area. It just so happened that the largest Martial Arts Business consulting organization in the country had its headquarters there too.

I decided to pay them a visit.

The day I visited they were scheduled to record a CD destined to be sent out to over 1,000 schools in over 12 countries. One of the people who was scheduled to be interviewed that day didn't show for the phone conference.

They asked me to take his place.

They put a microphone in my face and asked me what I thought made me unique as a teacher. I got that deer in the headlights look. I froze.

What felt like minutes, but probably was only a few seconds of silence I thought of something. I told them about my daily habit of always trying to make everywhere I go a little better. I told them about the theatre and wiping down the sink in the bathroom.

They kept my interview in. They published the CD.

My story went out to over 1,000 schools.

At the annual convention people came up to me and shook my hand. They pointed at me and said: "Hey, you're the wipe down the sink guy!"

The Chairman of the Association liked my interview. He was so impressed he made me an Advisory Board member to the largest Martial Arts Association in the world.

He opened countless doors for me. My relationship with his organization changed my business and my life.

When you do little things to help the world around you and take your mind off your own problems you are blessed in unimaginable ways.

Always be the one to wipe down the sink.

How To Create The "Wipe Down The Sink" Habit

Each day before you go to bed ask yourself the simple question: "Who or what did I make better today."

By asking yourself this question before you go to sleep you will program your unconscious to start looking for ways to serve throughout the day. As you serve you will turn your attention away from your own problems. When you turn your attention away from your own challenges (just like a mosquito bite) they will diminish.

Main Ideas Of Chapter 6

- Refuse to join in battles of any kind.

- Instead of trying to love negative things it's often better to simply remove yourself or change the subject.

- Conflict is romanticised in our culture; but conflict is always counter productive and pulls us away from love.

- Negative thinking is destructive; it will affect your balance and your actions.

- Make everywhere you go a little better.

SMT Exercises

- "Sneak out the back". Turn your attention away from conflict and negativity. Find any excuse, take a different rout, go to the bathroom. Find any reason to get away.

- "The 15 second rule". When you detect negative emotions practice turning your attention away in the first 15 seconds.

- "Wipe down the sink". Each night before going to bed ask yourself who or what you've made better today.

CHAPTER 7: Ego

You Are Losing

You we're taught that if you fought hard enough against your problems they would get better. You believed if you only worked harder you would succeed.

So you started the game of "Whack a Mole". But every time you smacked down one problem it get replaced with another. You got tired, you got reckless, you almost lost hope.

You didn't know that everything that was coming to you was coming because of your emotions. Every time you focused on a problem you we're creating it's emotional equivalent - and the emotions you created were causing the problem to pop up continuously.

You didn't know that focusing on your problems was the problem.

Everything in this first book is designed to do one thing. Take your focus away from anything that causes you negative emotion. Remember it's the negative emotion that draws to you experiences that are just like it. Your goal is to go through as much of your day as you can feeling good.

Happiness is not the result of what happens to you. Happiness is a skill that requires practice. Internal SMT is a group of techniques that can train anyone into the mental state of joy.

When you are experiencing the emotion of joy; joy will become your new point of attraction. Your life will begin to attract the events and things that are joyful. Good things happen not to those that wait; good things happen to those that are filled with love.

"There are no happy endings at the end of unhappy stories." - *Esther Hicks and the "Teachings of Abraham"*

Who Are You?

Imagine you are in a travel agency looking at all the pictures of places to go. Some of the places look fun, some look scary, some look expensive. Just because you look at the pictures doesn't mean you are buying a trip. The pictures are free; but when you get out your credit card, that's when your trip becomes real.

When you think without focusing you are only sampling. You are sifting through various possibilities with every image in your mind. But these images do not become real until you power them up. In SMT you are learning how to power up what you want, and pull the battery out of what you don't.

The energy that supplies your difficulties is your words - your narrative - what you say over and over again. Words - both audible and inaudible - are focused thought. When you learn to choose your words carefully you will be able to control the direction of your life.

You are not your thoughts, you are not the words you speak. Instead you are the one that chooses. You are a unique combination of both desire and choice. We call this combination your ego.

Never in the history of the world has there been nor will there ever be another person with the same combination of desire and choice.

For generations forms of meditation, martial arts and other practices have recommended destroying your ego. This is based on the belief that desire is the cause of all suffering. If you eliminate the part of you that wants you will stop your pain.

It's easy to see why you might want to be rid of desire. You've wanted certain things for so long that every time you think of them it hurts. It's natural to think that maybe you'd be better off without wanting anymore. But if you wanted to get rid of all desire wouldn't it just be easier to just jump off a bridge? Destroying the ego - no matter what method - is not the answer.

Positive Ego VS. Negative Ego

Ego is a unique combination of desire AND choice.
Everyone has desire. When you try to fulfill your desire with any motivation other than love you are operating from "negative ego". You are operating from "positive ego" when your desire is coming from love.

When spiritual teachers talk negatively about ego they are really talking about "negative ego". Negative ego wants you to sacrifice what you want so that it can have what IT wants. Negative ego wants to be in charge, to rule, to be king. It wants to win over, or control others. Negative ego is motivated by fear.

One form of ego always seeks love - and in so doing becomes unimaginably powerful. The other form of ego is a lie; it's mission is to trick you into sacrificing your happiness in its quest for power.

It could be said that your success or failure lies 100% with whichever form of ego you operate from. In this world there is only one kind of failure possible; unhappiness. There is also only one kind of success available - joy. If you operate from negative ego you always lose - even if you gain money, prestige, and victory in the short run. If you operate from positive ego (love) you always win.

Simply put: Negative ego wants to trade love for power. Positive ego surrenders power for love.

Ego came knocking on my door.
Love answered.
No one was home.
- Wayne Dyer

Everyone needs guidance. Most people use the quest for power as their compass. Only the enlightened few are led by love.

Forms of teaching that demand that you destroy your ego often forget the distinction between positive and negative ego. Your mission is not to get rid of desire; but instead to so nurture love that it becomes your constant guide.

Trying to get rid of your ego (desire) fails for one major reason. Usually the desire to get rid of ego is motivated by NEGATIVE EGO. (You only want to be rid of it because you think it will make you "better than" or "one up" over others).

Ego is simply the part of you that wants - ego is your DESIRE. How you go about getting those things is what counts. When you use love as your guide you create happiness in all directions.

In an ancient text, Jesus was asked which was the greatest of the ten commandments.

He replied:

"Thou shalt love the Lord thy God with all thy heart, and with all thy soul, and with all thy mind. This is the first and great commandment. And the second is like unto it, Thou shalt love thy neighbour as thyself. On these two commandments hang all the law and the prophets". —Matthew 22:37-40

Ask yourself dozens of times each day; "Is this thing I'm about to do motivated by love?" If the answer is no you are being guided by negative ego.

Sometimes others want you to give up your desires so they can recruit you to help them get what THEY want. When people behave this way they are operating from negative ego; and they are trying to convince your negative ego to follow them.

The greatest atrocities in human history were all based on convincing people to sacrifice love for some egotistical cause or another.

Create from love. Use your desire to hone the choices you make; always directing them towards love. Look at your desire as the path; and love as the light that shows the way. When you operate from desire and choose love you cannot ever be controlled by another and your life will be filled with joy.

Main Ideas In Chapter 7

- Happiness is not the result of what happens to you. Happiness is a skill that requires practice.

- Your ego is a combination of BOTH your desire and your decisions.

- Negative ego is when you act on a desire without love.

- Positive ego is when you act on your desire with love.

SMT Exercise

- Practice living by positive ego. Ask yourself each time you make a decision - "Is what I'm about to do motivated by love?"

CHAPTER 8: Frankenstein

You Have Created Monsters!

I was broke.

I created a monster. It was called "Poverty". It lived an independent life; but it needed to eat.

It's food was worry.

Every time I worried about money, every time I checked my bank account, every time I discussed how high an expense was, my monster fed.

The more I fed my monster, the more it came to visit.

At last, I stopped feeding it.

I stopped looking at money, stopped looking at bills, stopped talking about finances.

My monster grew weak. I prospered.

It's Alive!!!

"When you name something you bring it into existence. When you describe it you give it life." - Unknown

You focus your mind through the words you use. Any time you use words either in your head or out loud you are focusing. The words you use determine how you feel about everything.

Words don't just go away after they are thought or spoken. Thoughts are like real living things - and are born on the back of the subjects you talk and think about. They do eventually fade if they are starved; but if you continue to feed them they grow larger and more powerful.

In hypnosis, when powerful thought forms are purposefully attached to an event or object it is called "anchoring". These anchors have massive power. If you've ever seen a stage hypnotist you can see the power of these anchors. People can be made to "stick" to the floor, or there bodies can become as strong as steel under hypnotic anchors.

Each time you make a mental statement about a subject you "stack" words onto it and create an anchor. As an example; when it starts to rain and you think: "Damn; I hate the rain" You have stacked one affirmation on top of rain clouds.

No big deal; one affirmation doesn't matter much; but it usually doesn't end with one. You repeat these kinds of affirmations over and over again, over time (and many rain clouds later) you actually blame the cloudy day for your depression. What you don't realize is that you practiced yourself into depression. Each time you see a dark cloud you reactivate those thousands of programmed words - then you feel depressed.

Had you, from a young age, always spoke positive words when it rained you would not experience the same depression. If you had said thousands of times: "I love rainy days"; rainclouds would make you happy.

What makes these "anchors" tricky is while they might have been the birthplace of your thought form, *once alive, thought forms are free to jump from subject to subject.* Think of the words you think as living creatures; they will go to wherever they can survive and thrive.

A thought form will never "jump" to a subject that cannot sustain it. If you absolutely love your dog; but you have created a hateful thought form about your landlord, the hate cannot attach itself to your dog. Every time you think of your dog you are starving your thought form of hate.

Your thought of hatred will try desperately to attach itself to anything it can to live. Even if you move and never see your landlord again your thought form lives on. It will try to feed on ANY touchy subject it can find - maybe the government; or maybe your ex.

If every time you open your wallet you think "I never have enough" you have created a "never enough" thought form. Later you might decide not to carry a wallet, but that won't free you. Your thought form will simply look for another place to live where it can be fed regularly. It might decide to attach itself to your bank account, your closet space, or even your appetite.

Just because you take care of one problem; the words you have created will pop up elsewhere unless they are deactivated.

You are like Dr. Frankenstein; you have created monsters. You must take responsibility for what you have created - otherwise your creations will find a way to survive without you and return.

The good news is your monsters are easy to deactivate.

Your monsters were created with your words; they also survive on your words. Every single time you complain about something you are inviting one of your previously created thought forms to feed. Stop complaining, both in your mind and out loud and your thought forms starve.

Momentum

You now see why the rich get richer and the poor get poorer. When something happens - and you focus on it with words - you are laying a foundation for more of the same in your future. If your words are good you create good thought forms; if your words are bad you create evil ones.

Most people go through their day thinking they are narrators. They think they are describing the things that are independently going on around them. Little do they know that they are creators; and the story they tell is actually creating their future.

Stop The Momentum And Reverse It

Negative words you have given birth to are like radiation. Radiation is invisible and needs a Geiger counter to discover it. The tool you use to detect your creations are your feelings.

If a negative thought form is being hosted by a subject you will know - because every time a negative thought form feeds, you will feel a negative emotion.

You are also creating positive thought forms. When you create them they live on too; and whatever subject they are hosted on will always bring you joy. The whole purpose of SMT is to learn how to create and feed your positive thought forms, while at the same time learning to starve your negative ones.

You will always get more of how you feel. The emotion you are feeling shows you what thought forms you have attached to every subject. The emotion you feel is a sure sign of what is coming in your near future.

Phobias

If you are afraid of spiders, just the sight of one causes your heart to race.

You might say: "I didn't say anything about how bad spiders are; I saw one and I got scared." But you were scared only because in the past someone taught you how to be afraid. Then you used your internal words to reinforce what you learned with practice. In a short time you didn't need the words to cause the feelings because the your words had a life of their own. Now all you need to do is see a spider and BAM; all those negative emotions come flooding in.

A fear of spiders isn't a big deal; but the negative thought form that lives around the subject IS. You can always call an exterminator to get rid of spiders; but if you don't take care of the underlying thought, your fear will just pop up somewhere else when the spiders are gone. (Maybe centipedes, or snakes. Maybe even your Mother in law).

You are the chooser of your words. It's your words that create and sustain everything in your life. The goal of SMT is to teach you how to deactivate the thoughts that are causing you pain and next to teach you how to create positive thought forms; on purpose.

Phase 1: Internal SMT Meditation

Most of the problems you have are continually being recharged and perpetuated by your constant repeated thoughts and words. When you stop recharging your problems they will fade and you will feel relief quickly.

After you learn to stop negative wording, in Book 2, you will learn "Phase Two: External SMT" You will learn techniques to start using words (thinking) again - but this time on PURPOSE. You will learn how to plant seeds of the things you want to manifest in your life. But you've got to learn to stop the thoughts that are injuring you first.

You will not be able to program positive thinking into your life while negative habits are still active. This is because you will still be getting negative results - and it's difficult to speak in a positive way in the face of negative events.

Two of the practices in internal SMT that work hand in hand are: SILENCE and MINDFULNESS MEDITATION.

Silence is the practice of refusing to speak or think WORDS. Mindfulness meditation is using a point of focus (usually the breath) to distract yourself from thinking and consequently to stop feeding any negative thought forms.

Silence: The Thought Cleanse

To practice silence you simply choose to be quiet. You choose not to speak for a period of time. Just keep your mouth shut for one hour and watch what happens.

Silence is like a body cleanse. You discharge all subjects; good and bad alike. By starting with a total cleanse there is no chance that you are accidentally still creating a place for a negative thought form to feed.

During your silence you will notice the urge to speak out on various subjects. You will feel the temptation to mutter different thoughts and opinions under your breath. Simply let the temptation go. Refuse to talk - no matter what.

Remind yourself that each time you speak you are recharging your current thought forms. These creatures live off of the words you speak; they need you to continue to speak in order to survive. Do not give in. Do not give them even one scrap.

Your problems cannot survive the power of your silence.

At first you will slip. But if every time you catch yourself you simply go back to your practice, over time you will slip less. Eventually you will be able to go for long periods without using words.

Generally you can do a complete "thought cleanse" in about 24 hours. You simply go a full day without saying a word to anyone and doing your best not to speak - even in your mind.

After you do your cleanse you will be very sensitive to every thought and word you speak. This is an excellent time to carefully reintroduce speaking; but only speak of subjects that bring you happiness and joy.

When you learn to discipline yourself with silence you will be able to create a new life with ease. Your silence has power.

Here are the steps to practice your thought cleanse.

Plan a full day of silence - at least 24 hours - and more if you can to do a cleanse.
After your cleanse make an effort to monitor your words - it will be easier at this stage because your words and the emotions they

generate will be highly visible. Make this practice of never speaking ill or in anger on any subject a life practice.

What you might not realize is you've been speaking and creating many positive things as well as negative ones. The reason your positive creations are not fully coming to the surface is your negative thought forms keep choking them out. When you eliminate the negatives you will often experience dramatic results. No additional action is required - because you've been setting the goals and doing the work for a long time. You just didn't realize you were sabotaging all the good you created - but now you know how to stop doing that.

SMT practice must be "on" all the time. Be aware of your emotions from moment to moment; day in and day out. It's a skill; but it can be learned and it is the most important skill you will ever learn.

A Little Change Makes A Big Difference

I remember reading somewhere that areas of high crime are caused by only a few people. A tiny percentage of people can completely destroy a neighborhood.

Your problem areas work the same way. There are only three or four subjects (thought forms) that are responsible for 90% of the problems you face in life. Weed out those subjects; stop feeding them and life gets better fast!

Life After Your Thought Purge

Go through your day and notice every time you start to feel a negative emotion. What are subjects that cause you discomfort? Try and figure out what the underlying thought form is that feeds off these subjects.

If you are afraid when you see your boss is your thought form "lack"? If you get angry when you see someone breaking the law could your thought form be: "injustice"?

Sometimes when you can see your thought forms on paper it's easier to recognize when you are feeding them. List all of the subjects you notice and then pay careful attention to the top three. Almost always these are the things you fill your day. These are the subjects thinking you think and talk about the most. As soon as you use silence to throw your top three offenders out of the neighborhood your problem rate will drop like a rock.

For example; if every time you spend money you get a feeling of loss in the pit of your stomach; the way you feel about money is a good thought form to deactivate. Simply decide you will no longer discuss, think about, or dwell on money. If you stop feeding your "I don't have enough" thought form; you will see your bank account swell - no investment or action from you is required.

Some of your problem areas have been with your for a long time; but remember you are constantly reinforcing them every time they come up. If you just stop reinforcing your problems with words they will evaporate. Your problems need your words to live.

Refuse to speak ill of anyone or anything - this is going to take discipline. But realize that every time you speak (in your mind or with words) you are actually casting a spell on yourself. The spell has no affect on what you are condemning; but this spell has an enormous affect on you. Only speak or think words that you want to be true.

Now you know how to stop your negative wording and starve the most chronic problems you face in life. You now know more than 99% of all the people who meditate in the world. Use this information with wisdom and watch your life unfold in the most amazing and miraculous way.

If you want; put this book down and never read another word. There is really nothing else you need. I'm writing more pages to share more ideas, and because it's fun; but you don't need anything else. You have it all.

Do a purge as soon as you can. Problems of the past will crumble and dissolve. Watch how the simple act of silence allows you to rise. When you let go of your words, you let go of your limitations.

Main Ideas of Chapter 8

- Words you speak or think with emotion create thought forms that behaves like living things.

- Your thought form survives by feeding off more of the emotion that created it.

- Your negative thought forms can move from subject to subject; and jump to any subject you feel negatively about. The more negative words and thoughts spoken the more powerful and habitual your form gets.

- Phobias are an example of the power of a thought form that has grown strong.

- To deactivate your thought form you must silence yourself of the words your negative thought forms lives on.

SMT Exercise

- SMT Exercise: Refuse to speak or think negatively about anyone or anything. This is an art and must be practiced over time.

- SMT Exercise: Do a "Thought Cleanse" by going at least 24 hours without speaking. During this time refuse to speak out loud. Try not to use words in your mind; let go of all opinions.

Chapter 9: Meditation

Stop Multitasking

When you are driving down the road, listening to music and drinking a cup of coffee, it feels like you are aware of all three activities at the same time. Instead what you are doing is quickly shifting your focus from one subject to another.

Your attention shifts so quickly that you think you are focused on all three things; but instead you are jumping from subject to subject; one at a time.

You give your attention to the road; then quickly switch to the music, then quickly back to the coffee, then back to the road. The more objects you include in your mental cue the less energy you have for any one of those subjects.

When your mind flashes from subject to subject you will be less effective in each area. The more subjects you are switching back and forth with, the less awareness you have in any one area.

If you are sipping coffee by yourself, and not engaged in anything else, you fully taste it. But if you split your thinking by multi tasking you begin to dilute your awareness of the flavor. If only ⅓ of your attention is on the coffee - then you are getting only ⅓ of the flavor.

As our lives become more and more complex we enjoy less and less of what we have. This is the reason color and sound seemed so much more vibrant when we we're kids. We were experiencing much more of life back then. Today our attention is divided between so many subjects simultaneously we rarely experience any one thing to its fullest.

Sometimes splitting your attention can be useful. For example; if you have to drive a long way it makes perfect sense to use that time to listen to a book or a lecture. The trouble with splitting your attention is it's over use. It's fine to multitask when you are driving through Kansas; but it's a mistake to split your attention when it's time to listen to your kids or spouse.

When you habitually multi task you you begin to lose some of the best things in life.

There are two ways you can tell if you've fallen victim to the addiction of overly splitting your attention.

First; if you generally feel like your life has lost some of it's zest as the years have progressed. This is NOT normal. This is almost universal; but it's not natural - it is simply the product of bad habits of thought.

Second; if you sit to meditate, and you find it very difficult to stay focused on one subject for more than a few seconds or minutes.

Almost everyone has suffered from the addiction of a divided mind; and this problem only gets worse with age. As most of us get older it seems like life is going faster and faster; but this seeming increase in the speed of life is yet another symptom that we've lost control of our mind.

Have you ever noticed that the easiest way to get through a tough job is to stay busy? The busier you stay the quicker your day will seem. The busier your mind is (that is the more subject you are multitasking on) the quicker each day will feel; your life will seem to fly by while you are missing most of it.

It's true that almost everyone feels they are losing there life bit by bit as they get older. But this process can be reversed.

Meditation is the tool that will teach you how to undo the habit of splitting your attention and get your life back.

When you learn to meditate you will turn back the hands of time to a place when you experienced more joy. Your days and weeks will slow, and your life will again become vibrant. Even your coffee will taste better.

Mindfulness Meditation

Up to now all of the techniques we've introduce I consider "informal". Informal because there is no set way of practicing and they must be done on your own as part of the daily practice of living. Mindfulness Meditation on the other hand is "formal" in that it is very specific, and can be practiced in groups as well as privately.

Three important points before you begin.

1st: You must understand the principles of the "Law of Attraction" as I explained earlier in this book. If you don't understand how your mind works, you won't really understand and benefit from meditation. You won't be able to tell if you are on the right track because you won't understand the relationship between your mind and the results you get in your life. You might go through a daily ritual; but you become like the gangster who goes to church every Sunday. He's attending the meetings; but he leaves the message at the door.

2nd: Meditation is not mystical or complex. You should be able to explain meditation to someone in one or two sentences. If you can't; reread this chapter until you can.

3rd: Formal Meditation is only one of many SMT techniques. It's vital and extremely important; but it's one of many techniques that when used together have a cumulative effect. If you only use meditation but disregard the other methods in this book your results will be limited.

It's a shame that one of the most important techniques for helping you achieve your goals is frequently taught in an environment that tells you that first; it's wrong to want things - and second, it tries to explain the practice in a way that makes it seem mystical and difficult.

When you want something, it's the whole of who you are that wants it. You are the Universe expressing itself - your desire is good. Proper meditation is easy and it's designed to help you deactivate your negative thoughts so that you can get a fresh start and live your dreams.

How To Meditate

Begin by sitting comfortably in a position with your back straight. I like to use my couch but I pull my legs up cross legged; it pushes my back up against the back of the sofa perfectly. The main thing is you are comfortable and in an alert position.

I like to place my hands palm up; there is no magical reason for this - however it's a unique position that you don't use frequently throughout the day - so for me hands in lap palm up becomes an anchor that helps my body remember it's time to meditate.

Gently close your eyes and begin to place your attention on your breath. Notice the inhalation, notice the gentle exchange notice the exhalation. Do your best to keep your mind totally focused on the breathing and not let it drift to other subjects.

Usually within the first minute two things will happen.

First: you will experience a feeling of an itch, cramp, or some other discomfort in your body. This is your mind's way of playing a trick on you. If you have an itch; and decide to go ahead and scratch it, in clever fashion your mind will MOVE your itch to another area. Your best bet is to get fully comfortable BEFORE you begin your meditation - and know that since you were fully comfortable the temptation to move is just your mind playing tricks.

Second: you will have thoughts that will wander in and pull your attention away from the breath. When this happens have an attitude that says: "No big deal". Each time your mind wanders simply catch yourself and go back to the breath. Do not try to fight against the thoughts; simply let them go and go back to breathing. With practice your ability to stay focused for longer periods will grow strong.

The most important thing for dealing with distraction is not allow them to hook to other things. If during your meditation you catch yourself thinking about dinner, do not criticize yourself for letting your mind wander - remember your criticism is another distraction. Don't make a big deal out of anything that interrupts you; simply go back to the breath. You will improve with practice.

Notes On Meditation

1. Use a five minute daily goal.

Five minutes because everyone can find an extra five minutes, and with only a goal of five minutes you can make meditation something you do every single day. There will be times when you meditate for longer periods because you have the time and it feels good - wonderful; but make your goal simply five minutes daily. The five minute goal gives you no excuses.

2. Meditate in the same place at the same time every day.

It's best to make your meditation a habit; not a decision. The easiest way to do that is to hook it to an already existing habit. For example; if you always drink two cups of coffee in the morning, decide to do your meditation as soon as you finish your second cup. After a few weeks of practice will have an automatic reminder when it's time to meditate.

3. Remember the purpose of meditation.

You are learning to focus your mind so that you can concentrate without jumping from subject to subject. It's this jumping from one thing to another that makes us less effective and takes away some of the best moments in life.

When the mind habitually and without knowing it jumps from subject to subject, it will often jump to negative thoughts and beliefs. It's this jumping to your negative thought forms that keep you from making progress in your goals. When you eliminate this jumping process you are able to keep your mind focused on what you want you will begin to move forward.

Notice the little improvements as you practice over the first month or two. You will be able to read longer without your mind wandering. You will be able to more enjoy movies you watch. You will notice flavors of food that you haven't tasted in some time. When you meditate your life gets better; notice and cherish those improvements.

Do not view meditation as some deep spiritual practice designed to lead you to enlightenment. It might be - but the simple reality is, meditation will make your life better TODAY. It will give you more joy, and increase your effectiveness in everything you do. It will allow you to slow down life and take more in, and in the end there's nothing more important than that. By meditating you are learning to fully enjoy the life you have been given.

There are other methods that automatically force you to practice this form of phase one SMT meditation. As I write this book, every word is written during meditation. I am concentrating so carefully on what I want to communicate that there is no room for me to begin talking. I'm concentrating; and every word is coming from a kind of joy. As I type I can feel a few of my own negative thought forms starving.

You already know what it feels like to do mindfulness meditation. Most physical workouts will give you the same kind of feeling - they force you to concentrate - and concentration only happens when thinking stops.

The feeling of exhilaration you get when you finish a martial art, a yoga workout, or even a run, is not so much about training. The euphoria is coming because you were forced to still your mind. Imagine how wonderful it will be when you can get that feeling of joy for large sections of your day, based on a decision instead of an activity.

Main Ideas In Chapter 9

- When you multitask you hurt your ability to be effective.

- The sensation of life moving faster and being less fun is a symptom of chronic multitasking.

- When your mind accidentally jumps from subject to subject you will often jump to subjects that keep you from your goals.

SMT Exercise

- Practice Mindfulness Meditation in order train yourself away from multitasking.

- Set a committed goal to meditate for five minutes every day.

CHAPTER 10: The Red Wolf

A great Indian Chief was asked how a person could be happy and prosper. He answered: *"On your shoulders are two wolves. One wolf is black; it continually whispers in your ear all of the reasons you will fail and should be afraid. On your other shoulder is a red wolf; this wolf is always telling you to be brave and that you will succeed."*

He said: *"These wolfs fight every day. The wolf that wins determines your life."*

The Chief went on: *"If you want to live a long and prosperous life you must do only one thing daily. - You must FEED THE RED WOLF!"*

Learning to feed the thoughts you want and deprive the ones you don't is easy to understand. I'm going to teach you how in this chapter.

While the understanding is easy; implementing the solution is going to take some effort and practice. The results will speak for themselves.

Feeding a thought is called THINKING. Feeding a thought that's good for you is POSITIVE thinking.

Having a thought is not the same thing as thinking. You have thousands of random thoughts each day. Everything you observe or remember is a thought. But thoughts in and of themselves have no power. You must feed them first.

You feed a thought by describing in in vivid detail and giving your thought MEANING.

For example; take a look at your smartphone. When you notice it, it becomes a thought. But this thought doesn't have any energy; it's neutral.

If you take that same thought (smartphone) and begin to feed it with a description, you give it power. Your thinking might go something like this:

"My phone has rounded corners and a good weight that makes it easy to hold in my hand. Someone did a nice job designing it. The screen is colorful and illuminated so I can use it at all times to see images of anything. My phone is connected to the internet and any question can be instantly answered. It has more processing power than the most powerful supercomputer on the planet just a few years ago. My smartphone allows me to connect with the entire world, to manage my life, and be entertained - yet it goes with me wherever I am and fits in my pocket."

Notice that this positive description begins to generate an emotion; the description fuels the ordinary thought "smart phone" and infuses it with a FEELING - in this case the feeling might be described as "appreciation".

So the thought "smartphone" has no power on its own. It is one of thousands of random thoughts that come and go as you go through your day. But as soon as you begin to describe it and fuel it with detail the more you power it.

The evidence of a powerful thought is emotion. You generate emotion by giving things vivid descriptions. Whatever emotion you are feeling is ALWAYS ATTRACTING the things and events that match it.

The Politician

Your day is filled with subjects. Some of those subjects are easy to describe in joyful terms; but other subjects are tough. Some of your tough subjects have been a problem for a long time. They are difficult for you to even think of without beginning to think and feel negatively.

Every time one of those negative subjects come up you begin to go down a dark hole by describing it. You've got to stop.

It's the description of the thought that fuels it; it's what it lives on. When a subject comes up that causes you fear or anger you have to learn to take away it's vivid description. You've got to learn to be more non-specific about your problem subjects. When you describe something in specifics the thought grows in power. When describe something with generalities the thought grows weak.

I'm no fan of politicians; but if you watch them carefully you will know how to use your thinking more effectively. When a politician is asked about something positive they have accomplished they will speak in the most specific terms imaginable. But watch when a politician is asked about a touchy subject. They describe things as generally as they can and only speak in broad terms.

Here's an example. Notice how the Mayor goes into detail when it comes to the first question. But when he's asked about a question that he's not as proud of he just gives general statements.

Reporter: *"Mr. Mayor; tell me more about the new bridge being built over the river"?*

Mayor: *"It's one of our biggest accomplishments yet! We've employed well over 100 workers for 22 months, it will be completed by September of this year, and will be among the most beautiful structures in the South. We estimate over 80,000 cars a day will be using it to transport goods and services to our area, causing a net gain in taxable revenues from the increase in commerce of 5.6 million a year. On the whole it's one of the biggest wins in our city's history."*

Reporter: *"Tell me about the latest 1% city sales tax increase"?*

Mayor: *"As you know all cities have to support the infrastructure that makes living in them possible. We believe that our quality of life will improve as long as we continue to provide great services to our residents. Our vision is on the future; and improving everyone's life is our main goal".*

Notice how the Mayor is really detailed in his answer to the first question. But the second question, about the tax increase, he answers by speaking in broad general terms. We might hate this tendency in our representatives; but they do it for only one reason. IT WORKS.

Going general works because it takes our attention away from anything negative. It works for politicians; but it also works for you. It's a great way to handle and defuse negative thoughts in your own life.

Here's how you rid yourself of negative thought.

When a touchy subject comes do your best to get off the subject. Sometimes you can't change the subject; so instead get as general as you can until you can let it go.

Have you ever wondered why "Time heals all wounds"? It's doesn't. Time itself does nothing!

If you are angry with someone; but a scientist was able to put you in a cryogenic freeze for 10 years, you would still wake up mad. But if you were awake for a full 10 years you would gradually find other things to distract you. Your problem would heal.

Healing takes place not because of time. Healing takes place when we begin to focus on our problems less. Techniques like "The Politician" are ways to focus on the problem less and diffuse its energy.

When you use the technique correctly it feels like many years have passed.

I used the technique of "The Politician" recently.

I was scared. I was threatened with a lawsuit. I felt the suit was unjustified and every time the subject got brought up I was filled with rage.

I would review in sharp detail all of my positions, arguments, and counterpoints. I rehearsed what I would say to the lawyers. I ashamed to say I even visualized using physical violence against them and their client.

And then I started to get sick. The anger and resentment I was generating was making me ill.

Then I surrendered.

No more argument, no more energy. Every time the subject got brought up I'd say something like: "Oh well, I've been in a lot of worse situations than this and things have turned out just fine, and this kind of thing has been going around a long time and I can't solve it today, and I don't have to deal with this now, in ten years will all be laughing about it."

Then I'd change the subject to something else.

I did this OVER and OVER again. It was hard at first; but I did it anyway.

Then my body healed itself.

Then the problem dissolved. We settled (For VERY LITTLE money.)

And the only time I've thought about it since then is as I write this just now.

You have subjects in your own life that you know will make you sick. You have got to find words to describe them when they come up that are so broad and general that they cause the subject to lose it's grip. When your painful subject loses it's grip, drop it; let go of it like the evil thing it is.

Here are some of the thoughts I use on a regular basis to defuse a subject:

- I don't have to solve this now. (Procrastinate ON PURPOSE)
- This has been going on a long time and will continue even when I'm not around.
- Things have been worse.
- Time heals everything.
- I'm turning this over to a higher power.
- It's a big planet; nothing that happens today is going to throw it out of orbit.
- If it's a person I'm angry at I try and imagine the day they were born, or the day they graduated, and how proud their parents were of them.

- Whenever I judge someone as deserving punishment I remember a scene from the movie "The Unforgiven". In the movie Clint Eastwood is playing a Gunfighter. He's talking to a kid about killing another human. Here's how it goes:

Eastwood as The Gunfighter: "Will Munny": *"It's a hell of a thing, killing a man. Take away all he's got and all he's ever gonna have."*
The Kid: *"Yeah, well, I guess they had it coming; didn't they? ... Didn't they?"*
Will Munny: (long pause) ... *"We ALL got it coming, kid."*

Do anything you can to come up with a thought that defuses the rampage you are starting on. As soon as the thought weakens - get rid of it.

If you start down the road of POSITIVE momentum that's a whole different thing. When you start on a positive subject get as detailed as you can. Think about it and talk about it more.

Negative rampages cause you to get sick. Positive rampages cause you to be well. Negative rampages make you sad. Positive rampages make you happy.

It is your detailed description that feed all thoughts; good or bad. The more you starve negative thoughts, and feed joyous ones the better your life.

Main Ideas Of Chapter 10

- Learn to feed the thoughts that support you and starve the ones that are injuring you.

- You can starve negative thoughts by thinking about them only in a general way.

- You feed positive thoughts by thinking more and more sharp details about them.

SMT Exercise

- "The Politician": Memorize a list of general statements or stories you can use when you start down a negative path. When you start to feel negative use your list to remember how to diffuse your momentum until you can drop the subject. When you become more general on a subject it is as if you are placing your problem many years behind you.

CHAPTER 11: Unconditional Love

Love Is Its Own Reward

Love never asks or expects anything in return. Love is not selling; love is always a donation.

The shortcut to unconditional love is to value how you feel above everything else. Be kind and loving simply for the sake of how it makes you feel. Love is it's own reward.

It's easy to love those that love us. It's easy to be kind to the kind. It's easy to be honest with the honest. But real power comes when we choose to love without condition.

When a rich person is near it's easy to be kind; but how do you treat the beggar? Character is determined not by how you treat the most important; but by how you treat the one everyone considers least important.

In the movie adaptation of Ronald Dahl's children's classic "Charlie and the Chocolate Factory" Charlie has to make a decision. He has been lied to and is now being cheated. At that moment he can decide to cheat too and get his revenge; or follow his unconditional integrity and do the right thing - anyway.

Charlie makes the decision to do what's right in his heart. Only after he follows his heart do his blessings show up. He ends up receiving far more than he ever dreamed possible.

This is fable, but the truth is life work exactly the same. When you stop expecting rewards and do what's right you are blessed.

In the ancient text the Master says: *"Give so that your right hand doesn't know what your left hand is doing."* In other words give in a way that doesn't ask the Universe to give you something in return. Instead; give just for the sake of giving.

Being unconditional means you offer your goodness for only one reason; because you relish in the joy that giving brings. This is unconditional love. This is power.

What About The Things I Want?

When you hear the idea of love it might be easy to object: "What about the things in life I want; do I have to give them up?"

Love is not about giving things up; it's about getting everything you've always wanted! All of the physical things you've ever wanted you have wanted for only one reason; because you believed you would feel good when you got them. Love is the shortcut; you can get the good feeling NOW - you don't have to wait until the stuff shows up.

But because when you love you feel good. The Universe will bring you the physical objects that match your feelings - automatically.

When you love you feel prosperous. The Universe brings you prosperity.

When you love you feel connected. The Universe brings you intimacy.

When you love you feel powerful. The Universe brings you power.

When you love you feel healthy. The Universe brings you health.

You can have your cake and eat it too.

By loving you get the feeling of joy now; and the feeling draws to you all the stuff you've ever wanted.

Most people have it backward. They prostitute their joy, thinking the sacrifice will eventually bring them what they want. They don't realize they are actually chasing those things away.

Here's the formula most people in the world use today.

Bad Formula

Action -----> Leads to Getting Stuff -----> Leads to Feeling Good

But in SMT we teach a *different* formula.

Good Formula

Love ---> Leads to Feeling Good --->Leads to Getting Stuff *(But not really caring as much about the stuff)*.

Security comes when you learn to operate from formula two. In formula number two you learn to generate your own joy. You never have to be afraid of loss; because your joy isn't coming from physical events and objects.

But remember the Universe can see right through you. You can't decide to walk the path of love so that the you will in turn get things. You can't fool the Universe; you can only receive when you make a decision to surrender; to practice goodness for goodness sake alone.

This is an art. This is a lifestyle. This is what SMT is ultimately about.

How To Love

To put this practice into action you must begin to focus on your feelings. You make your feelings your goal, your highest priority.

Discipline yourself from moment to moment. Ask yourself continually how you feel. Any time you feel bad it means something has your attention that is pulling you away from love.

When you love all fear is gone.

Love is the most powerful process in this book. Love is the key to joy, abundance and health.

Learn to love without condition.

SMT is the art of unconditional love.

CHAPTER 12: Pulling It All Together

SMT methods are taught as an evolving system. SMT techniques are based on the principles of the Law of Attraction. SMT covers two important phases

Phase One - Where you learn to STOP the negative thought forms you have accidentally created or picked up. (Book 1)

Phase Two - Where you create thought forms on purpose that serve you. There are many techniques for creating more of what you want. (Book 2)

This book was all about phase one as it lays the foundation for phase two. Phase one gives you great benefit because when you stop thinking about certain subjects you will stop charging them. In a very short time many of the problems you are facing will fade.

Learning to keep your mind pointed in the right direction is an art. It's like getting fit; there are many different ways to do it - but you've got to keep at it if you want lasting results. You will have plenty of plateaus along the way. Just keep working at it; you will be glad you did.

These skills are practices. You get better by working on them.

List Of The Techniques In This Book

- **"One Pointedness"**: Remember the value in feeling good. Any time you feel a negative emotion rise discipline yourself to turn your attention to a more positive subject

- **Forgive Others:** Practice forgiveness. Picture the person from the past who hurt you on Christmas morning as a child; know that this is who they really are.

- **Stories:** Create stories that support how you want to feel. Ignore whether or not the stories are true. Joy does not require truth; joy is simply a story you tell.

- **Sleep:** Get enough sleep (at least eight hours)

    o Last Five Minutes: Take special care of the last five minutes before you drift off to be grateful and find joy so that you can take this state into your unconscious.

    o Wake: When you wake lay in bed a few minutes and remember all that you are grateful for. Then decide to hold onto your feeling of appreciation throughout the day.

- **"Sneak out the back":** Walk away from conflict and negativity. Find any excuse, take a different rout, go to the bathroom. (find any exit you can).

- **"15 second rule":** Turn your attention away from any negative emotion. If you can catch it in the first fifteen seconds you can stop it.

- **"Wipe Down the Sink":** Make every where you go a little bit better

- **"The Politician":** Memorize a list of general statements or stories you can use when you start down a negative path. When you start to feel negative use your list to remember how to diffuse your momentum until you can drop the subject.

- **Watch Your Words:** Refuse to speak or think negatively about anyone or anything. This is an art and must be practiced over time.

- **Silence:** Do a "Thought Cleanse" by going at least 24 hours without speaking. During this time refuse to speak, and try to not use words in your mind. Repeat this process every month or two.

- **Meditate:** Practice Mindfulness Meditation in order train yourself away from multitasking and deactivate negative thoughts. Set a committed goal to meditate for five minutes every day.

- **Love:** The basis of all SMT is love. Practice kindness and love daily. Make love your life's work. You don't need anything else.

Thank You

I hope you liked this book. I've shared the best lessons I know about deactivating negatives from your life.

If you've like it and it's been helpful to you I would love to have your review. You can review my book at the link provided on the last page. I promise I will read your review and use your feedback (positive or negative) to help my writing get better.

I've also been working hard on Book 2. Book 2 details how to actively use your mind to achieve your goals. The manuscript is finished and is now in the editing stage. It will be available on Amazon in 2016.

Epilogue

Yesterday I wrote the last word of this book. At least that's what I *thought*.

I had worked on it for months - hundreds of hours. I told no one; not even my wife.

Yesterday I felt the exhilaration I had heard of but never experienced. The feeling of a first book coming to a close and knowing it was DONE.

I let out a deep breath scooted away from the computer and said out loud: "finished!"

I thought smiling: "It's official; I'm now a part of a published work".

I went for a walk and started thinking about how to promote my book. Should I try public speaking again? Out of the blue I remembered a talk I'd given a few years earlier for a financial firm.

"Ugh" I thought; "not my best work; I think I'll send everyone a copy of my book to make up for it.". I was thinking that the talk didn't live up to my usual standards.

I thought of something else. It's very personal. I'm not going to include it here but it made what happened next all the more amazing..

One hour later I got a text from an acquaintance: Tim Croak. (Tim just happened to be one of the dozen or so people present at my talk a few years earlier).

Tim had never called me or sent a text before.

Here's his text:

"Hey joe, This is tim croak, I am having a book come out soon and I put a section in there about you and wanted to make sure it was ok. It is about the talk you gave to the agency a couple of years ago. I can send you the section if you want to see it."

I had NO idea Tim had been working on a book of his own. He had NO idea I was writing one either.

Crazy....

I got up this morning, my habit is to start every morning with something inspirational. I started listening to a random YouTube video. It's was a talk from Neale Donald Walsch. I haven't read or heard any of his stuff for several years. His talk was incredible and left me inspired.

My inbox dinged.

Tim had sent me the full manuscript for his amazing first book titled: *"The Light"*.

I opened Tim's book right at the prologue page. The first sentence quotes who inspired the title of this book? - Who else? - *Neale Donald Walsch!*

Tim talks about me on page 49.

Tim's book brought tears to my eyes. You need to read it.

Something beautiful and mysterious is going on in this world. We are connected. What we are putting out we are getting back. There are no accidents.

Life is magic.

About The Author

Joseph L. Hurtsellers is the creator of both "SMT meditation" and the "SMT system of Martial Arts". He is the author of *"Break The Chain" - books 1 & 2.* He is also the founder the Martial Arts Center in Maumee Ohio. He lives in Ohio and (sometimes) Arizona, with his life and business partner Shelly Blanco. Joe loves to teach his style of SMT Martial Arts. and takes his greatest pleasure in seeing other people use it as a tool to live healthier, happier and more productive lives.

Learn more about Joe at:

www.ohiomartialarts.com/sensei-joseph-hurtsellers

Also By Joseph Hurtsellers

Break The Chain! - Book 2 - External SMT
Available March 2016

More To Come...

One Last Thing...

If you enjoyed this book or found it useful I'd be very grateful if you'd post a short review on Amazon. Your support really does make a difference and I read all the reviews personally so I can get your feedback and make this book even better.

If you'd like to leave a review then all you need to do is go my books page and click the review button:

www.ohiomartialarts.com/breakthechain

Thanks again for your support!

Made in the USA
Lexington, KY
09 September 2018